Breaking Through the Clouds

THE SOMETIMES TURBULENT LIFE OF METEOROLOGIST JOANNE SIMPSON

Written by
Sandra Nickel

Illustrated by
Helena Perez Garcia

ABRAMS BOOKS FOR YOUNG READERS • NEW YORK

By the time Joanne was five, she had discovered her mother didn't much care where she was. That summer on Cape Cod, she slipped a small boat into the inlet behind her cottage, tipped her face to the sky, and watched the clouds above her. There were whiffs and ribbons and mountains of clouds. Some were brilliant; some were frightening. Joanne loved them all.

By the time Joanne was ten, she had learned her
mother's words could be icier than the coldest winds.

You are too stubborn. You are too smart.
You have to be loveable to be loved, Joanne.

When the words became too harsh, Joanne sailed
into the ocean and lost herself beneath the changing skies.

When her mother's silences grew stormier than the sea's
worst squalls, Joanne found a new way to lose herself.

She flew so high her wings almost touched the clouds.

As soon as Joanne was old enough, she flew far away, to the University of Chicago. The year before, World War II had broken out, and one of the world's greatest meteorologists had come to Chicago to help with the war. Carl-Gustaf Rossby knew everything about the great weather-making winds. He gave Joanne a crash course and asked her to teach weather officers going to war.

Joanne taught the men about the great winds, but she also warned them about the puffy white clouds she loved so much. They were called *cumulus* if there was one cloud and *cumuli* if there were more. The clouds held heat and moisture and could be bumpy inside. If at all possible, it was best not to fly into the biggest of them all, the cumulonimbus.

By the time World War II ended, Joanne had fallen so much in love with the science of weather that she wanted to become a doctor of meteorology like the great Carl-Gustaf Rossby.

Joanne, however, wanted to study clouds.

When the men at the university heard Joanne's plans, they laughed. Clouds were only currents of air filled with tiny beads of water, no more important than the steam lifting off their coffee. Rossby told Joanne to go home. He didn't need her anymore. Another professor said, "No woman ever got a doctorate in meteorology. And no woman ever will."

As Joanne walked through the university, the halls were filled with jarring comments and bumpy silences. She flew her last flight and sold her boat—because Joanne was stubborn.

Even if no professor would help her, she now had enough money to keep studying.

When summer came, Joanne returned to Cape Cod. She had heard the Woods Hole Oceanographic Institution had films of cumulus clouds. She asked if she could stay at Woods Hole for a week, and once there, she watched the films over and over. Clouds were born, grew, and floated on the wind. But as she watched, Joanne noticed something strange. The clouds seemed to be moving in their own ways. Misty air showed their trails behind them. What was going on?

Joanne went back to Chicago and bought a notebook. For over a year she did calculations,

studied the ideas of others,

and wrote ideas of her own.

At last, she came to an amazing conclusion. Cumulus clouds weren't just currents of air filled with tiny beads of water. They had energy. They could pull in dry air and push out moist air—and as they did, they could move in ways different from the wind.

When Joanne presented her work to the professors, they were so impressed, the university gave Joanne a doctorate of meteorology. She was the first woman in the world to receive one. As they draped the university's maroon-and-black regalia over her shoulders, Joanne felt as if she were flying higher than the clouds themselves.

Joanne organized an expedition with Woods Hole to take a closer look at clouds. She talked the U.S. Navy into loaning her a pilot and loaded one of their planes with instruments to measure temperature, wind speed, and moisture.

When everything was ready to go, the top scientists at Woods Hole suddenly announced that Joanne couldn't fly with the expedition. "No women allowed," they said. "It's Woods Hole policy."

Joanne was as stunned as if lightning had struck her out of the blue.
She couldn't study clouds in a test tube or under a microscope.
She *had* to be up in that plane.

Joanne turned to the U.S. Navy.

The officer in charge told Woods Hole, "It's Joanne's project. No Joanne, no plane." The top scientists didn't like it. They blustered and rumbled like distant thunder. But they let Joanne go.

For the next few years, Joanne flew under clouds, above clouds, and through clouds. She even flew into the most frightening clouds of all, the enormous cumulonimbi, full of gusting wind and pelting rain. As she took pictures and films, the rest of her team recorded the clouds' temperatures, their moisture, the wind speed, and more. Joanne also bought a new sailboat and watched the clouds grow and disappear from below.

Back on land, Joanne wrote her discoveries in her notebooks and drew maps of clouds, showing for the first time how clouds move across the sky. She also began telling the world about cumulus clouds. Just like people, cumulus clouds are born, grow, and die. But unlike people, they exist for no longer than two hours. They don't float on air like a bubble, but pull in air from beneath them. And the faster the air rises, the more turbulent the clouds become.

Not everyone was open to what Joanne had to say. Plenty still thought women shouldn't be meteorologists. Plenty still thought clouds were unimportant. "No one else is interested in clouds," said Rossby.

Stubborn as always, Joanne started watching cumulonimbi build day and night over the warmest oceans. Some of them grew to an enormous ten miles tall, higher than the trade winds—and that got Joanne thinking. She examined the heat and moisture inside and outside of the clouds and once again discovered something incredible.

These clouds had massive power. They carried ten times as much energy as the atomic bombs used in World War II. And they thrust their heat into the high altitudes. These enormous puffy white clouds weren't just dynamic, moving in ways different from the weather-changing winds. They were *powering* the winds. No one could say clouds were unimportant now.

Joanne knew so much that she was now ready to create a mathematical model to show how clouds grow. If she succeeded, scientists would be able to put current weather conditions into the model and predict how clouds would react in the future. Rossby had already made a model for predicting how global-scale currents of warm and cold air move across the earth, but he had one of the world's first computers. It was so big it took up nearly an entire building.

Joanne had a pencil, slide rule, and graph paper. She had erased so many times her paper was filled with holes. But Joanne wasn't about to give up.

One day, Rossby came to Woods Hole to visit other scientists. When he saw Joanne's work on her cloud model, he changed his mind about clouds and Joanne. He invited her to use his gigantic computer. He told her, "You are making a big contribution after all."

It took Joanne two years, but she finished her cloud model. It was the first of its kind and sparked an entire branch of science. Soon, scientists began designing new models to give us the predictions we are so used to today: *partly sunny skies, showers in the morning, expect blue skies in the afternoon.*

Thirty years later, the American Meteorological Society elected Joanne the president of them all. There were still harsh winds and squalls along the way, but Joanne never stopped going up in plancs. She never stopped sailing. And she never stopped telling the world about the puffy white clouds she loved so much.

You don't just sit there and all of a sudden
a light bulb flashes over your head and you say, "Aha!"
What you have to learn to be is . . . stubborn.

—*Joanne Simpson*

Author's Note

Throughout her life, Joanne Simpson went out of her way to support young meteorologists, especially women. She helped them understand how weather works and inspired them with her enthusiasm and generosity. One young meteorologist, who prospered thanks to Joanne, said Joanne didn't simply blaze a trail for women, "she blazed a road." Joanne was so well-known for helping others that the American Meteorological Society named an award after her: the Joanne Simpson Mentorship Award.

Joanne wrote in her notebooks almost every day and reread her ideas time and again. Her first ten notebooks—where she writes about getting her doctorate, flying with Woods Hole, discovering the power of clouds, and creating the first cloud model—are held in the Arthur and Elizabeth Schlesinger Library at Harvard University.

Joanne wrote nearly two hundred articles about clouds. One of her most famous, written with Professor Herbert Riehl, her colleague for many years, showed that cumulonimbus clouds not only power the trade winds with their enormous heat, they also power hurricanes.

Joanne won medal after medal, including two of the most important awards in meteorology: the Carl-Gustaf Rossby Research Medal and the International Meteorological Organization Prize. The National Air and Space Administration (NASA) named one of its supercomputers after her.

When Joanne was sixty-three years old, NASA put her in charge of the first satellite to track rain and storms in the tropics, the Tropical Rainfall Measuring Mission. She had already observed clouds from land and sea and air. Now, with the help of the satellite's images, Joanne examined clouds from outer space, working until she died in 2010.

My thanks to Dr. Margaret A. LeMone, former president of the American Meteorological Society, for her invaluable insights about Joanne Simpson and helping me get things right about clouds.

Joanne Simpson with her Woods Hole team and the U.S. Navy plane, 1952

Joanne studying results of her flights at Woods Hole, 1959. Two of her notebooks sit on the counter in front of her.

Joanne taking films of clouds, circa 1969

Selected Bibliography

Atlas, David and Margaret A. LeMone. *Joanne Simpson.* National Academies Press, Memorial Tributes: Volume 15 (2011).

Berczuk, Carol. *Choices and Successes: Honoring Women Pioneers.* Annals of the New York Academy of Sciences, vol. 869, issue 1, April 1999.

Eldridge, Larry. *Persistence Lifted the Clouds. Christian Science Monitor*, October 30, 1989.

Houze, Robert A. Jr. *From Hot Towers to TRMM: Joanne Simpson and Advances in Tropical Convection Research.* Meteorological Monographs, vol. 29, no. 51.

LeMone, Margaret. *Stories Clouds Tell.* Boston: American Meteorological Society, 1993.

Remembering Joanne Simpson: A Life of a Legendary Meteorologist. Atmos News, March 5, 2010.

Rice, Doyle. "Meteorology Pioneer Joanne Simpson Dies." *USA Today*, March 9, 2010.

Simpson, Joanne. Interview by Margaret LeMone. American Meteorological Society, tape-recorded interview project, September 6, 1989.

———. *Meteorologist.* Annals of the New York Academy of Sciences, vol. 208, issue March 1, 1973.

———. *Cloud Photographs—Beauty and Information, Pacific Cloud Hunter 1952.* Joanne Simpson Collection, Schlesinger Library, Radcliffe Institute, Harvard University (1994. MC 779, Box 2).

———. *Overview of Childhood, 6 months to 8 years.* Joanne Simpson Collection, Schlesinger Library, Radcliffe Institute, Harvard University (1994. MC 779, Box 1).

———. *Notebook One: Joanne Simpson, Development of Ph.D. Dissertation, August 1947–June 1949.* Joanne Simpson Collection, Schlesinger Library, Radcliffe Institute, Harvard University (1994. MC 779, Box 9, File 3).

———. *Notebook Six: Joanne Simpson, 1955–1957, England, Sweden and Start of the Pacific Investigation.* Joanne Simpson Collection, Schlesinger Library, Radcliffe Institute, Harvard University (1994. MC 779, Box 10, File 4).

———. *Preface to Papers of Joanne Simpson.* Joanne Simpson Collection, Schlesinger Library, Radcliffe Institute, Harvard University (1994. MC 779, Box 9).

Tao, W.-K., et al. *The Research of Dr. Joanne Simpson: Fifty Years Investigating Hurricanes, Tropical Clouds, and Cloud Systems.* Meteorological Monographs, vol. 29, January 2003.

Weier, John. *Joanne Simpson.* NASA Earth Observatory, April 23, 2004.

Timeline of Joanne Simpson's Life

1923   Born in Boston, Massachusetts, on March 23

1933   Sailed solo for the first time at age ten

1939   Flew solo for the first time and received her pilot's license at age sixteen

1949   Earned the title of doctor of meteorology, the first woman in the world to do so

1957   Completed the world's first cloud model

1983   Awarded the Carl-Gustaf Rossby Research Medal, the first woman to win the American Meteorological Society's highest honor for atmospheric science

1986   Appointed as lead scientist for the Tropical Rainfall Measuring Mission, the first weather satellite to track rain and storms in the tropics

1989   Elected president of the American Meteorological Society

2002   Awarded the International Meteorological Organization Prize, the first woman to win the World Meteorological Association's highest honor

2010   Died on March 4

To Kate and Chris, who started it all
—S.N.

For my parents and for Pablo,
and for all those girls and women
who aren't afraid of flying high
—H.P.G.

The illustrations in this book were made with gouache.

Cataloging-in-Publication Data has been applied for
and may be obtained from the Library of Congress.

ISBN 978-1-4197-4956-8

Text © 2022 Sandra Nickel
Illustrations © 2022 Helena Perez Garcia
Book design by Jade Rector

Photos opposite Author's Note courtesy Schlesinger Library,
Radcliffe Institute, Harvard University.

Printed and bound in China
10 9 8 7 6 5 4 3 2 1

Abrams Books for Young Readers are available at special discounts when
purchased in quantity for premiums and promotions as well as fundraising or
educational use. Special editions can also be created to specification. For details,
contact specialsales@abramsbooks.com or the address below.

ABRAMS The Art of Books
195 Broadway, New York, NY 10007
abramsbooks.com